Crypto Clarity: Navigating the World of Digital Investments

In a world that's constantly evolving, the financial landscape is no exception. The rise of cryptocurrencies has left many investors feeling uncertain and bewildered. But fear not, for "Crypto Clarity: Navigating the World of Digital Investments" is here to guide you through this exciting but often perplexing terrain.

This comprehensive book is your indispensable companion on the journey to understanding and profiting from digital investments. With clear language and a straightforward approach, it demystifies the complex world of cryptocurrencies and blockchain technology.

The book begins by laying a solid foundation, explaining what cryptocurrencies are and how they work. You'll gain a firm grasp of the fundamental concepts, such as blockchain, decentralized networks, and cryptography, without drowning in technical jargon. This knowledge is crucial for anyone looking to venture into the world of digital investments.

Once the basics are firmly established, "Crypto Clarity" delves into the various cryptocurrencies available today. It provides insights into the most prominent players like Bitcoin and Ethereum, as well as emerging alternatives. You'll learn about their unique features, use cases, and potential for growth, enabling you to make informed investment decisions.

Risk management is a central theme throughout the book. Whether you're a seasoned investor or just starting, you'll find invaluable advice on how to navigate the volatile crypto market.

In addition to cryptocurrency investments, "Crypto Clarity" explores other facets of the digital finance world. It covers topics like Initial Coin Offerings (ICOs), tokenization, and decentralized finance (DeFi), all of which have the potential to reshape traditional financial systems.

Furthermore, the book provides guidance on how to store and secure your cryptocurrencies, addressing concerns about digital wallet safety and best practices for safeguarding your assets.

To ensure you're well-prepared for the future, "Crypto Clarity" also delves into the regulatory landscape surrounding cryptocurrencies. It discusses the evolving legal framework and its implications for investors and businesses operating in the crypto space.

In summary, "Crypto Clarity: Navigating the World of Digital Investments" is your compass in the vast sea of digital finance. It provides a clear, accessible, and comprehensive roadmap for understanding, investing in, and profiting from cryptocurrencies. Whether you're a novice or an experienced investor, this book equips you with the knowledge and tools needed to navigate this exciting and transformative financial landscape with confidence. Prepare to embark on a journey of financial discovery and potential prosperity with "Crypto Clarity" as your trusted guide.

Key Topics:

- Introduction to cryptocurrency and blockchain technology in simple terms.
- Understanding the different types of cryptocurrencies and their use cases.
- Navigating cryptocurrency exchanges and wallets securely.
- Evaluating the potential risks and rewards associated with crypto investments.
- Strategies for building a diversified cryptocurrency portfolio.
- Exploring emerging trends in decentralized finance (DeFi) and non-fungible tokens (NFTs).
- Overcoming common misconceptions and myths about cryptocurrency.
- Staying updated with regulatory changes and market developments.

Chapters:

Introduction

At the inception of the internet age, few could foresee the profound changes it would usher in. From the first email to the advent of online shopping, the digital landscape has been continuously transforming our lives. Nevertheless, one of the most remarkable outcomes of this digital era has been the emergence of cryptocurrencies.

Cryptocurrencies, commonly referred to as "crypto," have garnered global attention. In this chapter, we will provide a comprehensive overview of their remarkable journey.

The Promise and Risks of Digital Investments

Cryptocurrencies stirred excitement by promising decentralized finance, global transactions, and financial inclusion. Many believed in the potential for these digital assets to revolutionize traditional finance. Bitcoin, the pioneer of cryptocurrencies, gained recognition as a digital store of value impervious to government interference. Ethereum, with its smart contract capabilities, hinted at broader applications beyond finance.

However, alongside these promises, cryptocurrencies brought forth a host of risks. Extreme price fluctuations, regulatory uncertainties, and scams raised legitimate concerns. The same speculative fervor that led to substantial gains also resulted in significant losses for unprepared investors.

The Need for Clarity: The Book's Purpose

In the middle of this excitement and uncertainty, it became evident that the world of cryptocurrencies lacked much-needed clarity. Misinformation, technical jargon, and the absence of reliable guidance left investors in a state of bewilderment.

The genesis of this book, "Crypto Clarity: Navigating Digital Investments," stemmed from this pressing need. Our primary goal is to demystify cryptocurrencies and provide a clear, accessible roadmap for digital investments. We aim to empower you with the knowledge and tools required to confidently navigate this exhilarating yet intricate landscape.

Our journey commences with the establishment of a solid foundation. We will elucidate what cryptocurrencies are and how they operate. We will unravel the complexities of blockchain technology and the cryptographic methods of securing digital assets. Additionally, we will trace the historical trajectory of cryptocurrencies, from the inception of Bitcoin to the present-day proliferation of diverse coins and tokens.

Subsequently, we will delve into the potential that cryptocurrencies hold. From decentralized finance to non-fungible tokens (NFTs) and tokenization, we will illustrate how these innovations are reshaping industries and presenting new investment opportunities.

Nonetheless, our focus extends beyond the allure of potential rewards; we will also confront the associated risks. Throughout the book, we will furnish you with practical risk management strategies, guidance on securing your digital assets, and insights into the regulatory framework governing cryptocurrencies.

Our objective is to equip you with the knowledge necessary to make informed decisions in the realm of digital investments. Upon concluding this book, you will possess a comprehensive understanding of cryptocurrencies, their potential, and the risks involved. Armed with this knowledge, you will be prepared to navigate the ever-evolving landscape of digital finance, seizing opportunities while safeguarding your financial future.

In this swiftly evolving landscape, clarity is your most valuable asset. "Crypto Clarity" serves as your guide, your companion, and your wellspring of insights as we embark together on this journey through the rise of cryptocurrencies and the pursuit of financial clarity.

Chapter 1: Decoding Cryptocurrencies

In this chapter, we embark on a journey to understand cryptocurrencies. To do that, we must first define what cryptocurrencies are and delve into the technology that underpins them: blockchain.

Understanding Cryptocurrencies: Defining cryptocurrencies and blockchain technology.
Understanding Cryptocurrencies

Cryptocurrencies are digital or virtual currencies designed to function as a medium of exchange. Unlike traditional currencies issued and regulated by governments, cryptocurrencies are decentralized. This means they operate on a technology called blockchain, a distributed ledger that records all transactions across a network of computers.

At the core, cryptocurrencies are based on cryptographic principles. These principles ensure that transactions are secure and that the creation of new units is controlled. The most famous cryptocurrency, Bitcoin, was created in 2009 by an anonymous individual or group using the pseudonym Satoshi Nakamoto. Bitcoin paved the way for a multitude of other cryptocurrencies, each with its unique features and purposes.

The Role of Blockchain Technology

Now, let's decode the technology that makes cryptocurrencies possible: blockchain. Imagine a digital ledger that records every transaction made with a cryptocurrency. This ledger is not stored in one place but is distributed across a network of computers, making it highly secure and resistant to manipulation.

Here's how it works:

1. Transactions: When you send or receive cryptocurrency, the transaction is broadcast to the network.
2. Verification: The network's nodes (computers) validate the transaction to ensure it's legitimate. This validation process often involves solving complex mathematical problems, a process known as mining.
3. Adding to the Blockchain: Once verified, the transaction is added to a block, which is a collection of transactions. Each block contains a reference to the previous block, creating a chain of blocks – hence the term "blockchain."
4. Decentralization: Copies of the blockchain are stored on many computers across the network. This decentralization ensures that no single entity can control or manipulate the ledger.
5. Security: Cryptography is used to secure transactions and control the creation of new units. Participants in the network have cryptographic keys, a public key for receiving

funds, and a private key for authorizing transactions.

6. Consensus: To maintain the integrity of the blockchain, the network must agree on the state of the ledger. This consensus is reached through various algorithms, such as Proof of Work (PoW) or Proof of Stake (PoS).

Key Takeaways

- Cryptocurrencies are digital or virtual currencies that operate on a decentralized network.
- Blockchain technology is the backbone of cryptocurrencies, providing a secure and transparent way to record transactions.
- Transactions are verified by a network of computers, and once validated, they are added to a chain of blocks, forming the blockchain.
- Cryptography is used to secure transactions and control the creation of new units.
- Consensus mechanisms ensure that the network agrees on the state of the ledger.

In summary, cryptocurrencies are digital currencies that rely on blockchain technology for their existence. Understanding these fundamental concepts is essential as we navigate the world of digital investments. In the following chapters, we will explore different aspects of cryptocurrencies, from their various types to their potential applications and risks.

The Bitcoin Genesis: Tracing the origins of the first cryptocurrency.

The Birth of Bitcoin

Bitcoin, the pioneer of cryptocurrencies, came into existence in 2009 when an individual or a group using the pseudonym Satoshi Nakamoto introduced it to the world. Nakamoto's whitepaper, titled "Bitcoin: A Peer-to-Peer Electronic Cash System," outlined the concept and the technology behind this groundbreaking digital currency.

The Need for Bitcoin

To grasp the significance of Bitcoin's emergence, we must first understand the challenges it aimed to address. Traditional currencies, also known as fiat currencies, are issued and regulated by governments and central banks. These institutions exert control over the supply and distribution of money. However, this control also means that currencies can be subject to inflation, devaluation, and the influence of political decisions.

In response to these challenges, Bitcoin was created as a digital alternative. It was envisioned as a form of currency that would operate independently of centralized authorities, providing users with greater financial control and security.

How Bitcoin Works

At the heart of Bitcoin's operation is a distributed ledger known as the blockchain, which we discussed in the previous chapter. Bitcoin transactions are recorded on this blockchain, ensuring transparency and security.

Here's a simplified explanation of how Bitcoin works:

- **Wallets:** Users have digital wallets that store their Bitcoin. Each wallet has a public key (like an account number) and a private key (like a password). The public key is used for receiving funds, while the private key is essential for authorizing transactions.
- **Transactions:** When someone wishes to send Bitcoin to another user, they create a transaction. This transaction is broadcast to the Bitcoin network.
- **Mining:** Transactions are verified by network participants, also known as miners. Miners use powerful computers to solve complex mathematical puzzles, a process that consumes energy and is known as mining. Once a miner successfully solves a puzzle, they validate the transaction and add it to a block on the blockchain.
- **Consensus:** To maintain the integrity of the blockchain, all participants must agree on the state of the ledger. This consensus is achieved through the Proof of Work (PoW) algorithm, where miners compete to validate transactions and secure the network.
- **Decentralization:** Copies of the blockchain are stored on numerous computers worldwide, ensuring that no single entity can control or manipulate the ledger.

Key Characteristics of Bitcoin

- **Decentralization:** Bitcoin operates without a central authority, making it resistant to government interference.
- **Limited Supply:** There is a maximum supply of 21 million Bitcoins, which creates scarcity and is designed to combat inflation.
- **Security:** The blockchain's cryptographic features make Bitcoin transactions highly secure.
- **Anonymity:** While transactions are recorded on the blockchain, users' identities are not directly tied to their public keys.

The Impact of Bitcoin

Since its inception, Bitcoin has sparked a global movement towards digital currencies and blockchain technology. It has given rise to a multitude of other cryptocurrencies, each with its unique features and purposes.

Bitcoin has also gained recognition as a store of value, often referred to as "digital gold." Some investors view it as a hedge against traditional financial instability and inflation, similar to how gold has been historically used.

Altcoins: Beyond Bitcoin

Diverse Crypto Landscape: Introducing various types of cryptocurrencies beyond Bitcoin.

While Bitcoin stands as the first and most well-known cryptocurrency, it is by no means the only one. A plethora of other digital currencies, often referred to as "altcoins" (alternative coins), have emerged over the years, each with its unique features and purposes.

Ethereum (ETH)

One of the most prominent altcoins is Ethereum. Launched in 2015 by Vitalik Buterin, Ethereum introduced the concept of "smart contracts." These are self-executing contracts with the terms of the agreement directly written into code. Smart contracts have far-reaching applications beyond digital currencies and can be employed in fields such as supply chain management and decentralized applications (DApps).

Ethereum's native currency, Ether (ETH), serves both as a digital currency and a fuel for executing smart contracts on the Ethereum network.

Ripple (XRP)

Ripple, often denoted by the symbol XRP, differentiates itself from Bitcoin and Ethereum by focusing on facilitating cross-border payments for financial institutions. Ripple's technology aims to expedite international money transfers, making them faster and more cost-effective.

Litecoin (LTC)

Litecoin, created by Charlie Lee in 2011, shares many similarities with Bitcoin. It is often referred to as "silver" to Bitcoin's "gold." Litecoin is favored for its faster transaction confirmation times and a different hashing algorithm, which makes it suitable for smaller, everyday transactions.

Bitcoin Cash (BCH)

Bitcoin Cash emerged in 2017 as a result of a "hard fork" from the original Bitcoin blockchain. It aimed to address some of Bitcoin's limitations, primarily by increasing the block size. This adjustment allows for more transactions to be processed in each block, potentially reducing transaction fees and speeding up confirmation times.

Stablecoins

In a space known for its price volatility, stablecoins provide a sense of stability. These cryptocurrencies are typically pegged to a stable asset, such as a fiat currency like the US Dollar (USD) or a commodity like gold. Tether (USDT) and USD Coin (USDC) are examples of stablecoins. They are used to facilitate trading on cryptocurrency exchanges and as a store of value when traders want to temporarily exit volatile markets.

Tokens and Tokenization

Tokens are a distinct category in the cryptocurrency world. Unlike cryptocurrencies like Bitcoin and Ethereum, tokens are often built on existing blockchain platforms, such as Ethereum. They represent various assets or have specific use cases within blockchain ecosystems.

For example, non-fungible tokens (NFTs) have gained prominence as unique digital assets. These tokens, often associated with art, collectibles, and virtual real estate, are indivisible and cannot be exchanged on a one-to-one basis.

Privacy Coins

Privacy coins, like Monero (XMR) and Zcash (ZEC), focus on enhancing user privacy and anonymity. They employ advanced cryptographic techniques to shield transaction details, making it difficult to trace the flow of funds on their blockchains.

Utility Tokens

Utility tokens grant access to specific features or services within a blockchain ecosystem. For instance, within the Ethereum network, tokens like Chainlink (LINK) provide data oracles, while Uniswap (UNI) tokens enable participation in decentralized exchange governance.

Chapter 2: The Mechanics of Blockchain

In this chapter, we unravel the inner workings of blockchain, the foundational technology that underpins cryptocurrencies. Understanding how blockchain functions is essential as we delve deeper into the world of digital investments.

Unveiling Blockchain: Explaining the foundational technology behind cryptocurrencies.

Blocks and Chains

A blockchain is a distributed ledger made up of a series of blocks, each containing a batch of transactions. Imagine a digital ledger that records transactions in a secure and immutable manner. These transactions could involve the exchange of cryptocurrencies or the execution of smart contracts. To maintain clarity and security, these transactions are grouped into blocks.

The term "blockchain" itself describes the structure of this technology. It's a chain of blocks, where each new block references the previous one, forming a continuous chain. This referencing ensures the integrity and chronological order of transactions.

Decentralization

One of the central tenets of blockchain technology is decentralization. Unlike traditional centralized systems, where a single entity or authority controls the ledger, blockchain operates on a decentralized network of computers, often referred to as nodes.

These nodes work together to validate and record transactions. Each node has a copy of the entire blockchain, ensuring that no single point of failure exists. This decentralized nature makes blockchain resistant to tampering and fraud.

Consensus Mechanisms

To add a new block to the blockchain, there must be a consensus among the nodes that the proposed transactions are legitimate. This consensus is achieved through various mechanisms, with the two most common ones being Proof of Work (PoW) and Proof of Stake (PoS).

- **Proof of Work (PoW):** In a PoW system, miners compete to solve complex mathematical puzzles. The first miner to solve the puzzle gets to validate the block and add it to the blockchain. This process is known as mining and is resource-intensive, requiring significant computational power.
- **Proof of Stake (PoS):** PoS, on the other hand, doesn't rely on mining. Instead, validators (equivalent to miners in PoW) are chosen based on the amount of cryptocurrency they "stake" as collateral. Validators are then responsible for validating transactions and securing the network.

Immutability and Security

Once a block is added to the blockchain, it becomes extremely difficult to alter or delete any of the information contained within it. This immutability is achieved through cryptographic hashing.

- **Hashing:** Each block contains a reference to the previous block's hash (a unique string of characters). Any change in the data of a block would alter its hash. Since each block references the previous one, changing a single block's data would require changing the data of all subsequent blocks, an impractical and nearly impossible task.
- **Security:** Cryptography plays a vital role in blockchain security. Transactions on the blockchain are secured using cryptographic keys. Users have a public key for receiving

funds and a private key for authorizing transactions. These keys ensure the privacy and security of transactions.

Transparency and Anonymity

Blockchain technology offers a unique balance of transparency and anonymity. On one hand, all transactions are recorded on the blockchain, making them visible to anyone with access to the network. This transparency is essential for trust and accountability.

On the other hand, user identities are not directly tied to their public keys, ensuring a degree of anonymity. Instead of revealing personal information, users are identified by their public keys, adding a layer of privacy.

Practical Applications Beyond Cryptocurrencies

While blockchain technology is most commonly associated with cryptocurrencies, its applications extend far beyond digital currencies. Here are a few examples:

- **Smart Contracts:** These self-executing contracts with the terms directly written into code have applications in industries like law, real estate, and supply chain management.
- **Supply Chain:** Blockchain can be used to track the production and distribution of goods, enhancing transparency and reducing fraud in supply chains.
- **Healthcare:** Medical records stored on a blockchain can improve data security and allow for efficient sharing of patient information.

- **Voting Systems:** Blockchain can be used to create secure and transparent voting systems, reducing the risk of fraud in elections.

Use Cases and Beyond Highlighting blockchain's potential in various industries beyond finance.

Use Cases and Beyond

Blockchain technology, originally devised to underpin cryptocurrencies, has demonstrated its adaptability and potential in numerous sectors. Let's delve into some compelling use cases beyond finance.

Supply Chain Management

One of the most transformative applications of blockchain lies in supply chain management. Traditional supply chains are often marred by opacity, inefficiencies, and susceptibility to fraud. Blockchain introduces transparency and traceability to these complex systems.

In a blockchain-based supply chain, each step of a product's journey is recorded as a transaction on the blockchain. This immutable ledger ensures that the origins, handling, and transportation of goods can be tracked with precision. If an issue or contamination arises, the affected product can be swiftly identified and removed from circulation.

Healthcare and Medical Records

In healthcare, the secure and interoperable management of medical records is of paramount importance. Blockchain technology offers a promising solution to the challenges of storing, accessing, and sharing medical data.

Patients' medical records can be stored as encrypted entries on a blockchain, accessible only to authorized healthcare providers. This approach ensures data security, reduces administrative overhead, and streamlines the sharing of medical information among various stakeholders, ultimately improving patient care.

Voting Systems

Blockchain has the potential to revolutionize voting systems by addressing concerns about security, transparency, and trust in elections. Blockchain-based voting systems can provide secure, verifiable, and tamper-proof methods for casting and counting votes.

Each vote is recorded as a transaction on the blockchain, and once recorded, it cannot be altered. Voters can verify their votes, enhancing confidence in the electoral process. Blockchain-based voting systems have the potential to increase voter turnout, reduce fraud, and make elections more accessible.

Intellectual Property and Copyright

Protecting intellectual property and ensuring artists, writers, and creators receive fair compensation for their work is a challenge in the digital age. Blockchain can establish transparent and immutable records of intellectual property rights and copyright ownership.

Digital content, such as music, art, and literature, can be registered on a blockchain, creating an indisputable record of ownership and usage rights. Smart contracts can automate royalty payments, ensuring creators receive compensation when their work is used or sold.

Real Estate and Property Records

Property records are often plagued by inefficiencies and disputes. Blockchain can bring transparency and security to real estate transactions and property records.

When property ownership is recorded on a blockchain, it becomes a matter of public record, easily accessible and verifiable by all parties. Smart contracts can facilitate property transactions by automating tasks like title transfers and escrow payments, reducing the need for intermediaries and simplifying the buying and selling process.

Food Safety and Traceability

Blockchain's transparent and immutable ledger is instrumental in ensuring food safety and traceability. In the event of a foodborne illness outbreak or contamination, blockchain can swiftly trace the origins of affected products, preventing their distribution and safeguarding public health.

Every step in the food supply chain, from farm to table, can be documented on a blockchain. Consumers can scan a product's QR code to access detailed information about its journey, including its source, processing, and distribution history.

Chapter 3: Investing Wisely in Crypto

We will explore the critical aspect of assessing risk and reward when venturing into cryptocurrency investments. Understanding the inherent volatility and potential returns in the crypto market is essential for making informed investment decisions.

Assessing Risk and Reward: Understanding the volatility and potential returns of crypto investments.

Assessing Risk and Reward

Investing in cryptocurrencies can offer significant opportunities for financial growth, but it comes with inherent risks. To make informed investment choices, it's vital to understand both the rewards and potential pitfalls.

Volatility in the Crypto Market

One of the defining characteristics of the cryptocurrency market is its volatility. Unlike traditional financial markets, where price fluctuations are relatively stable, cryptocurrencies can experience extreme price swings in a short period. This volatility can be attributed to several factors:

1. **Lack of Regulation:** The absence of regulatory oversight in the early days of cryptocurrencies

contributed to wild price fluctuations. Although regulatory frameworks have evolved, the market remains more volatile than traditional markets.

2. **Market Sentiment:** Cryptocurrency prices are heavily influenced by market sentiment, news, and social media trends. Positive news can drive prices up, while negative news can lead to rapid declines.

3. **Speculation:** Many investors enter the crypto market with speculative intentions, aiming to profit from short-term price movements. This speculative nature intensifies volatility.

4. **Liquidity:** The liquidity of many cryptocurrencies is relatively low compared to established assets like stocks or bonds. Lower liquidity can lead to more significant price swings.

Potential Returns

While the crypto market's volatility presents risks, it also offers the potential for substantial returns. Over the years, cryptocurrencies like Bitcoin and Ethereum have delivered remarkable gains for early investors. Here are a few reasons why:

1. **Early Adoption:** Those who invested in cryptocurrencies during their infancy have witnessed exponential growth. As cryptocurrencies gain mainstream acceptance, early adopters have reaped the rewards.

2. **Limited Supply:** Some cryptocurrencies, like Bitcoin, have a capped supply. This scarcity can drive up demand and, consequently, prices.

3. **Technological Innovation:** Blockchain technology, the foundation of cryptocurrencies, has the potential to revolutionize various industries. Investors believe in the transformative power of blockchain, driving investments.

Risk Management Strategies

Given the inherent volatility of cryptocurrencies, risk management is crucial for prudent investors. Here are some strategies to consider:

1. **Diversification:** Spreading investments across multiple cryptocurrencies can help mitigate risk. Diversification reduces exposure to a single asset's price fluctuations.
2. **Risk Tolerance:** Assess your risk tolerance before investing. Only allocate funds you can afford to lose. Cryptocurrency investments should not compromise your financial stability.
3. **Research:** Conduct thorough research before investing in any cryptocurrency. Understand the technology, team, use case, and market dynamics of the assets you choose.
4. **Long-Term Perspective:** Consider a long-term investment horizon. Short-term price fluctuations may be dramatic, but cryptocurrencies have shown the potential for substantial long-term gains.
5. **Use of Stop-Loss Orders:** Implement stop-loss orders to limit potential losses. These orders automatically sell a cryptocurrency when it reaches a predetermined price.

6. **Stay Informed:** Keep up with cryptocurrency news and market developments. Being informed helps you make informed decisions and react to market changes.

Market Cycles

Cryptocurrency markets tend to move in cycles, characterized by periods of bullish (upward) and bearish (downward) trends. Recognizing these cycles can be instrumental in making strategic investment choices.

1. **Bull Markets:** Bull markets are characterized by rising prices and widespread optimism. Investors often experience substantial gains during these periods. However, it's crucial to exercise caution and avoid excessive speculation.
2. **Bear Markets:** Bear markets involve falling prices and pessimism. While they can be challenging, they also present buying opportunities. During bear markets, investors often accumulate assets at lower prices, anticipating future growth.
3. **Market Corrections:** Corrections are temporary reversals in an asset's price during an ongoing bull market. These are healthy for the market, allowing it to cool off after rapid gains.

Different Investment Approaches: Exploring trading, holding, and other investment strategies.

Different Investment Approaches

Investing in cryptocurrencies offers a spectrum of approaches, each with its own set of principles and goals. Let's explore the most common strategies:

1. **HODLing (Hold On for Dear Life)**

HODLing is a long-term investment strategy where investors buy cryptocurrencies and hold onto them for an extended period, often irrespective of short-term price fluctuations. The term "HODL" originated from a misspelled "hold" in a Bitcoin forum post and has since become a symbol of steadfast commitment to a cryptocurrency.

Why HODL?

- **Long-Term Gains:** HODLers believe that over time, the value of their cryptocurrency holdings will appreciate significantly, leading to substantial profits.

Considerations for HODLing:

- **Patience:** This strategy requires patience and a willingness to endure market volatility without panic-selling.
- **Research:** Thoroughly research and select cryptocurrencies with strong fundamentals and promising long-term potential.

2. **Day Trading**

Day trading involves buying and selling cryptocurrencies within the same trading day, aiming to profit from short-term price movements. Day traders closely monitor market trends and use technical analysis to make rapid trading decisions.

Why Day Trade?

- **Short-Term Gains:** Day traders aim to capitalize on daily price volatility, potentially generating profits in a short timeframe.

Considerations for Day Trading:

- **Risk Management:** Day trading is high-risk and can lead to significant losses. Use stop-loss orders and never invest more than you can afford to lose.
- **Skill and Experience:** Successful day trading requires a deep understanding of market patterns and technical analysis.

3. **Swing Trading**

Swing trading falls between HODLing and day trading in terms of time horizon. Swing traders aim to profit from price swings that occur over several days to weeks, rather than within a single day.

Why Swing Trade?

- **Opportunistic Gains:** Swing traders look to capitalize on short-to-medium-term market fluctuations, aiming for more substantial gains than day traders.

Considerations for Swing Trading:

- **Technical Analysis:** Like day traders, swing traders use technical analysis to identify entry and exit points.
- **Risk Management:** Swing trading carries risks, so it's essential to manage risk effectively.

4. Scalping

Scalping is an ultra-short-term trading strategy where traders make a large number of small, quick trades to profit from tiny price movements. Scalpers aim to capitalize on market inefficiencies and bid-ask spreads.

Why Scalp?

- **Quick Profits:** Scalping offers the potential for numerous small profits throughout the day, accumulating to a substantial gain.

Considerations for Scalping:

- **Speed and Precision:** Scalping requires rapid decision-making and execution. It's not suitable for inexperienced traders.
- **Costs:** Frequent trading can incur higher transaction costs.

5. Value Investing

In cryptocurrencies involves identifying undervalued assets and holding them for the long term. Investors seek cryptocurrencies with strong fundamentals, solid use cases, and potential for growth.

Why Value Invest?

- **Fundamental Analysis:** Value investors believe that cryptocurrencies with strong fundamentals will eventually be recognized by the market and experience price appreciation.

Considerations for Value Investing:

- **Research:** In-depth research is essential to identify undervalued assets.

- **Patience:** Value investing typically involves holding assets for an extended period, often through market fluctuations.

6. **ICO and Token Sales Participation**

Participating in Initial Coin Offerings (ICOs) and token sales involves investing in newly issued cryptocurrencies before they are listed on exchanges. This approach allows investors to access potentially groundbreaking projects at an early stage.

Why Participate in ICOs and Token Sales?

- **Early Entry:** Investors can enter projects at an early stage, potentially benefiting from significant price appreciation.

Considerations for ICO and Token Sales Participation:

- **Research:** Thoroughly research projects, teams, and whitepapers before participating.
- **Risk:** Early-stage investments are risky, and not all projects succeed.

7. **Staking and Yield Farming**

Staking involves locking up cryptocurrencies in a blockchain network to support its operations. In return, investors receive rewards in the form of additional tokens. Yield farming, on the other hand, involves providing liquidity to decentralized finance (DeFi) protocols in exchange for rewards.

Why Stake or Yield Farm?

- **Passive Income:** Staking and yield farming offers the potential for passive income in the form of additional tokens.

Considerations for Staking and Yield Farming:
- **Network and Protocol Selection:** Choose reputable networks and protocols to stake or farm.
- **Risks:** Understand the risks associated with locking up assets and providing liquidity.

Due Diligence: Research and Factors to Consider: Highlighting the importance of research and analysis before investing.

Due Diligence: Research and Factors to Consider

Investing in cryptocurrencies can be lucrative, but it is accompanied by a degree of risk. To make well-informed and prudent investment choices, thorough research and consideration of key factors are paramount.

Understanding the Technology

Before investing in any cryptocurrency, it is crucial to understand the underlying technology. Each cryptocurrency operates on a unique blockchain or platform with distinct features and use cases. Consider the following:

- **Blockchain Type:** Is the cryptocurrency based on a proof-of-work (PoW) or proof-of-stake (PoS) blockchain? Understanding the consensus mechanism is vital.
- **Use Case:** What problem does the cryptocurrency aim to solve? Assess whether the project addresses a real-world issue and has a clear use case.

- **Development Team:** Investigate the background and expertise of the development team. Are they capable of executing the project's vision?
- **Community and Adoption:** Evaluate the size and activity of the cryptocurrency community. High community engagement can be a positive indicator of adoption.

Market Capitalization and Liquidity

Market capitalization (market cap) is a key metric that reflects the total value of a cryptocurrency. It is calculated by multiplying the current price per coin by the total number of coins in circulation. Understanding a cryptocurrency's market cap can provide insights into its size and potential for growth.

Additionally, assess the liquidity of the cryptocurrency. Liquidity refers to how easily an asset can be bought or sold without causing significant price fluctuations. Higher liquidity typically means a more stable market.

Risk Assessment

Cryptocurrency investments inherently involve risk. It is essential to assess and manage these risks effectively. Consider the following factors:

- **Price Volatility:** Cryptocurrencies are known for their price volatility. Understand that prices can fluctuate significantly in a short period.
- **Regulatory Risks:** Be aware of the regulatory environment in your jurisdiction. Regulatory changes can impact the legality and taxation of cryptocurrency investments.

- **Security Risks:** Safeguard your investments by using secure wallets and exchanges. Understand the risks associated with different storage options.
- **Scams and Fraud:** Be cautious of fraudulent schemes and phishing attempts. Exercise diligence when evaluating investment opportunities.

Investment Horizon and Goals

Define your investment horizon and goals clearly. Determine whether you are looking for short-term gains, long-term growth, or passive income through staking or yield farming. Your investment strategy should align with your objectives.

- **Short-Term:** If seeking short-term gains, you may engage in active trading or participate in ICOs and token sales.
- **Long-Term:** For long-term growth, consider HODLing cryptocurrencies with strong fundamentals.
- **Passive Income:** If aiming for passive income, explore staking, yield farming, or lending platforms.

Diversification

Diversification is a risk management strategy that involves spreading your investments across multiple cryptocurrencies. It can help reduce the impact of poor-performing assets on your overall portfolio.

Consider diversifying across different types of cryptocurrencies, such as established coins like Bitcoin and Ethereum, and smaller-cap altcoins.

Diversification can provide a balanced risk-reward profile.

Stay Informed

The cryptocurrency market is dynamic and ever-evolving. Stay informed about market trends, news, and developments in the blockchain and crypto space. Being up-to-date can help you make timely investment decisions.

Chapter 4: Navigating Crypto Exchanges

Understanding the functions and significance of exchanges is crucial for anyone venturing into the world of cryptocurrencies.

The Role of Exchanges: Explaining how crypto exchanges facilitate trading.

The Role of Exchanges

Cryptocurrency exchanges serve as the primary infrastructure for buying, selling, and trading digital assets. They are the digital counterparts of traditional stock exchanges but with distinct characteristics tailored to the unique nature of cryptocurrencies.

Facilitating Asset Exchange

At its core, a cryptocurrency exchange is a digital platform that brings together buyers and sellers of digital assets. It acts as an intermediary, providing a secure and efficient marketplace for users to trade various cryptocurrencies. Here's how it works:

- **User Registration:** To start trading on an exchange, users typically need to create an account. This process involves identity verification to comply with regulatory requirements.
- **Deposits:** Users deposit their desired cryptocurrencies into their exchange wallets. These wallets are specific to the exchange and hold the assets available for trading.
- **Order Placement:** Users can place different types of orders, including market orders (buying or selling at the current market price) and limit orders (buying or selling at a specific price). These orders are matched with those of other users on the exchange.
- **Order Matching:** The exchange's order matching engine matches buy and sell orders based on price and other parameters. Once a match is found, the trade is executed.
- **Execution:** Upon execution, the traded assets are transferred from the seller's wallet to the buyer's wallet within the exchange. The exchange acts as an escrow to ensure the transaction's integrity.
- **Withdrawals:** Users can withdraw their assets to external wallets for added security or long-term storage.

Variety of Cryptocurrencies

Cryptocurrency exchanges offer a wide variety of digital assets for trading. While some exchanges primarily list popular cryptocurrencies like Bitcoin and Ethereum, others provide access to a broader range of altcoins (alternative cryptocurrencies). The availability of diverse assets allows traders to explore different investment opportunities.

Marketplace for Altcoins

Altcoins encompasses all cryptocurrencies other than Bitcoin. Many exchanges cater specifically to altcoin trading, providing a platform for investors to discover promising projects. Some altcoins aim to address specific use cases, such as privacy, smart contracts, or decentralized finance (DeFi).

Exchange Types

There are various types of cryptocurrency exchanges, each designed to cater to different user needs. The primary exchange types include:

- **Centralized Exchanges (CEXs):** These are the most common type of exchanges, characterized by a central authority that manages trading operations. CEXs offer a user-friendly interface, high liquidity, and a wide range of assets. However, they require users to trust the exchange with their funds.
- **Decentralized Exchanges (DEXs):** DEXs operate without a central authority, allowing users to trade directly from their wallets using smart contracts. DEXs prioritize user control

and privacy but may have lower liquidity and a more limited selection of assets.

- **Hybrid Exchanges:** Some exchanges combine elements of both centralized and decentralized models. They offer the convenience of centralized exchanges while allowing users to maintain control of their private keys.

Security Measures

Security is a paramount concern in the cryptocurrency space due to the irreversible nature of transactions. Cryptocurrency exchanges implement various security measures to protect user funds and data, including

- **Cold Storage:** Storing a significant portion of funds offline in cold wallets, which are less susceptible to hacking.
- **Two-Factor Authentication (2FA):** Requiring users to provide two forms of verification (e.g., a password and a mobile app code) to access their accounts.
- **Insurance Funds:** Some exchanges maintain insurance funds to compensate users in the event of a security breach.
- **Regulatory Compliance:** Adhering to regulatory standards to ensure user protection and comply with anti-money laundering (AML) and know-your-customer (KYC) regulations.

Liquidity and Trading Pairs

Liquidity is a measure of how easily an asset can be bought or sold without affecting its price significantly. Exchanges with high liquidity typically offer tighter spreads (the difference between the buy and sell prices) and more favorable trading conditions.

Trading pairs represent the combinations of cryptocurrencies that can be traded against each other. Common trading pairs include BTC/USD, ETH/BTC, and LTC/ETH, among others. The availability of diverse trading pairs allows traders to explore various market opportunities.

Popular Exchanges: Overview of prominent exchanges and their features.

Popular Exchanges

Cryptocurrency exchanges come in various shapes and sizes, each with its own unique characteristics. Here, we introduce some of the well-known exchanges in the market.

1. Binance

- **Overview:** Binance is one of the largest and most popular cryptocurrency exchanges globally. It offers a wide range of trading pairs and services, making it a go-to choice for both beginners and experienced traders.
- **Features:**
    - **Extensive Asset Selection:** Binance offers a diverse selection of cryptocurrencies, including major coins and a multitude of altcoins.
    - **High Liquidity:** The exchange boasts high liquidity, enabling users to execute trades quickly.
    - **Advanced Trading:** Binance provides a user-friendly interface for beginners and

an advanced trading platform for experienced traders.

- **Binance Coin (BNB):** Binance has its native cryptocurrency, BNB, which users can use to pay for trading fees at a discounted rate.

2. Coinbase

- **Overview:** Coinbase is known for its user-friendly interface and is often the first choice for those new to cryptocurrencies. It is a regulated exchange based in the United States.
- **Features:**
  - **Beginner-Friendly:** Coinbase is designed with beginners in mind, offering a simple and intuitive user interface.
  - **Secure Wallet:** The exchange provides a secure wallet for storing digital assets.
  - **Educational Resources:** Coinbase offers educational resources to help users learn about cryptocurrencies.
  - **Regulatory Compliance:** It adheres to U.S. regulations, providing a sense of security for users.

3. Kraken

- **Overview:** Kraken is a reputable exchange known for its robust security measures and wide range of supported cryptocurrencies. It has a strong presence in both the United States and Europe.

- **Features:**
    - **Security:** Kraken is renowned for its security measures, including cold storage of funds and two-factor authentication (2FA).
    - **Margin Trading:** It offers margin trading for experienced traders looking to amplify their positions.
    - **Fiat Integration:** Kraken provides fiat currency funding options, **making it easier to deposit and withdraw funds.**

4. Bitstamp

- **Overview:** Bitstamp is one of the longest-standing cryptocurrency exchanges, established in 2011. It is known for its reliability and strong emphasis on regulatory compliance.
- **Features:**
    - **Security:** Bitstamp prioritizes security, implementing rigorous measures to protect user funds.
    - **Regulated:** It is one of the few regulated exchanges, providing a level of trust for users.
    - **User-Friendly:** Bitstamp's user interface is straightforward, making it accessible for both beginners and experienced traders.

5. Huobi

- **Overview:** Huobi is a global cryptocurrency exchange with a strong presence in Asia. It offers a wide range of cryptocurrencies and trading pairs.

- **Features:**
  - **Variety of Cryptocurrencies:** Huobi lists numerous cryptocurrencies and tokens, catering to diverse trading preferences.
  - **Staking:** The exchange offers staking services, allowing users to earn rewards on supported assets.
  - **Advanced Tools:** Huobi provides advanced trading tools and options for professional traders.

6. Gemini

- **Overview:** Gemini is a U.S.-based exchange founded by the Winklevoss twins. It focuses on regulatory compliance and security.

Features:

- **Regulated:** Gemini is fully regulated in the United States, providing a high level of compliance and security.
- **Institutional Services:** The exchange offers services tailored to institutional investors, including custody solutions.
- **Mobile App:** Gemini's mobile app is user-friendly and allows for trading on the go.

7. KuCoin

- **Overview:** KuCoin is a cryptocurrency exchange known for its wide range of supported cryptocurrencies and competitive trading fees.

- **Features:**
  - Extensive Asset Selection: KuCoin lists numerous altcoins, making it suitable for those interested in less well-known projects.
  - KuCoin Shares (KCS): KuCoin has its native cryptocurrency, KCS, which can be used to reduce trading fees.
  - Liquidity: The exchange provides reasonable liquidity for most trading pairs.

8. Bittrex

- **Overview:** Bittrex is a U.S.-based exchange known for its security and commitment to regulatory compliance.
- **Features:**
  - Security: Bittrex places a strong emphasis on security, implementing industry best practices.
  - Regulation: The exchange complies with U.S. regulations, offering a regulated trading environment.
  - Stablecoins: Bittrex offers various stablecoins, which can be useful for trading and minimizing exposure to crypto market volatility.

Security Measures: Discussing the importance of choosing secure and reputable exchanges.

Security Measures

The security of your digital assets should be of paramount concern when navigating the crypto exchange ecosystem. The decentralized nature of cryptocurrencies means that once they are transferred, they cannot be easily recovered if stolen. Therefore, selecting exchanges with robust security measures is imperative.

Importance of Security

Cryptocurrency exchanges act as custodians of your digital assets while they are on the platform. Entrusting an exchange with your assets means you rely on them to safeguard your holdings from theft, fraud, and cyberattacks. Here's why security matters:

- **Protection Against Hacks:** Secure exchanges implement rigorous security protocols to prevent unauthorized access and hacking attempts. They employ encryption, firewalls, and intrusion detection systems to safeguard user data and funds.

- **Risk Mitigation:** A secure exchange reduces the risk of losing your assets due to security breaches. The loss of digital assets can have severe financial consequences and can be irreversible.

- **Trust and Reputation:** Reputable exchanges prioritize security and compliance with regulatory standards. This commitment to security builds trust among users and the broader crypto community.

Security Features to Consider

When evaluating the security of a cryptocurrency exchange, consider the following key features and practices:

- **Cold Storage:** Secure exchanges store a significant portion of user funds in offline wallets, often referred to as cold storage. These wallets are not connected to the internet, making them less susceptible to hacking.
- **Two-Factor Authentication (2FA):** 2FA adds a layer of security by requiring users to provide two forms of verification (e.g., a password and a one-time code from a mobile app) to access their accounts.
- **Withdrawal Whitelists:** Some exchanges allow users to create withdrawal whitelists, specifying the addresses to which withdrawals can be sent. This prevents unauthorized withdrawals to unknown addresses.
- **Regular Security Audits:** Reputable exchanges undergo regular security audits conducted by third-party cybersecurity firms. These audits assess the platform's security measures and identify vulnerabilities.
- **Insurance Funds:** Certain exchanges maintain insurance funds to compensate users in case of a security breach or loss of funds due to exchange-related issues.

Regulatory Compliance

Security extends beyond technical measures and encompasses regulatory compliance. Trustworthy exchanges adhere to regulatory standards and implement Know Your Customer (KYC) and Anti-Money Laundering (AML) procedures to verify user identities.

- **User Verification:** Users are required to verify their identities through government-issued identification documents, proof of address, and other verification steps.
- **AML Policies:** Exchanges have AML policies in place to monitor and report suspicious transactions to regulatory authorities.
- **Compliance with Local Laws:** Reputable exchanges comply with the regulatory requirements of the jurisdictions in which they operate. This ensures legal protection for users and adherence to local financial regulations.

Reputation and Track Record

An exchange's reputation and track record are invaluable indicators of its security. Consider the following factors:

- **User Feedback:** Research user reviews and feedback about the exchange's security practices and customer support. User experiences can provide insights into an exchange's reliability.
- **History of Security Incidents:** Investigate whether the exchange has experienced security

incidents or hacks in the past. A history of breaches may indicate vulnerabilities.

- **Transparency:** Trustworthy exchanges are transparent about their security practices and measures. They often publish information about their security protocols and insurance coverage.

Due Diligence

Before entrusting an exchange with your digital assets, conduct due diligence. Research the exchange thoroughly, understand its security practices, and assess its reputation. Consider the exchange's regulatory compliance, security features, and track record of security incidents.

Chapter 5: Wallets and Security

We'll explore various types of wallets, including hardware, software, and paper wallets, to help you make informed choices in protecting your crypto holdings.

Types of Wallets: Exploring hardware, software, and paper wallets.

Types of Wallets

Cryptocurrency wallets are essential tools for managing and safeguarding your digital assets. These wallets come in various forms, each with its own set of advantages and considerations. Let's explore the three main types of wallets:

1. Hardware Wallets

Hardware wallets are physical devices designed specifically for securely storing cryptocurrencies. They are considered one of the most secure options for safeguarding digital assets. Here's an overview of hardware wallets:

- **Offline Storage:** Hardware wallets are offline storage devices, meaning they are not connected to the internet when not in use. This isolation significantly reduces the risk of online attacks.
- **Private Key Protection:** Private keys, the cryptographic keys required to access and manage your cryptocurrencies, are stored securely within the hardware wallet. They never leave the device, making them immune to online threats.
- **User-Friendly:** Hardware wallets often feature user-friendly interfaces, making them accessible to both beginners and experienced users.
- **Cost:** While hardware wallets offer top-tier security, they come at a cost, as you need to purchase the physical device.

2. Software Wallets

Software wallets, also known as hot wallets, are applications or software programs that run on your computer, smartphone, or other devices. They are convenient for everyday transactions but require careful consideration of security aspects:

- **Accessibility:** Software wallets are easily accessible on devices you use regularly, making them convenient for managing your cryptocurrencies.
- **Private Key Storage:** Software wallets store your private keys on the device where the wallet is installed. While they provide flexibility, this can make them vulnerable to malware or hacking if your device is compromised.
- **Variety of Options:** There are numerous software wallets available, ranging from mobile wallets for smartphones to desktop wallets for computers. Some even offer multi-platform compatibility.
- **Security Measures:** To enhance security, use reputable software wallets with strong encryption and password protection. Regularly update your software to patch any security vulnerabilities.

3. Paper Wallets

Paper wallets are a form of cold storage and offer a high level of security for long-term storage of cryptocurrencies. They involve generating a physical paper representation of your private and public keys:

- **Offline Storage:** Similar to hardware wallets, paper wallets are stored offline, protecting your keys from online threats.
- **Minimal Attack Surface:** Since paper wallets are physical and do not rely on software or digital devices, their attack surface is minimal.

- **DIY Creation:** You can generate a paper wallet yourself using various online tools, making it a cost-effective option.
- **Physical Vulnerabilities:** While paper wallets are secure from digital threats, they are susceptible to physical damage, loss, or degradation over time. Properly store your paper wallet in a secure and dry location.

Choosing the Right Wallet

Selecting the right wallet depends on your specific needs and preferences. Here are some considerations to help you make an informed choice:

- **Security:** If security is your top priority and you plan to hold a significant amount of cryptocurrency, consider using a hardware wallet or paper wallet for long-term storage. Reserve software wallets for small, everyday transactions.
- **Convenience:** Software wallets offer convenience for daily use but may have slightly lower security compared to hardware and paper wallets. Determine the balance between convenience and security that suits your needs.
- **Backup and Recovery:** Understand the backup and recovery options provided by your chosen wallet. This is essential in case your device is lost or damaged.
- **Multi-Platform Compatibility:** If you frequently access your cryptocurrency across multiple devices, consider wallets that offer compatibility across various platforms.

- **Regular Updates:** Keep your software wallet updated with the latest security patches to minimize vulnerabilities.
- **Reputation:** Research and select wallets with a strong reputation for security and reliability.

Protecting Your Investments: Discussing security measures, including two-factor authentication and cold storage.

Protecting Your Investments

Cryptocurrency investments are vulnerable to a range of security threats, including hacking, phishing attacks, and fraud. To mitigate these risks and protect your investments, consider the following security measures:

1. Two-Factor Authentication (2FA)

Two-factor authentication is a fundamental security feature that adds an extra layer of protection to your cryptocurrency accounts. It requires users to provide two forms of verification before granting access. Here's how it works:

- **Password:** The first factor is something you know—a password or PIN.
- **Authentication Code:** The second factor is something you have—an authentication code generated by a mobile app like Google Authenticator or received via SMS.

Advantages of 2FA:

- **Enhanced Security:** 2FA significantly reduces the risk of unauthorized access, even if someone knows your password.

- **Phishing Protection:** It helps protect against phishing attacks, where malicious actors attempt to trick you into revealing your credentials.

Implementing 2FA:
- **Enable 2FA:** Most cryptocurrency exchanges and wallets offer 2FA as an option. Enable it in your account settings.
- **Secure Backup:** Store backup codes securely in case you lose access to your authentication device.
- **Avoid SMS 2FA:** While SMS-based 2FA is better than no 2FA, it can be less secure than app-based options due to SIM swapping attacks.

2. Cold Storage

Cold storage refers to storing your cryptocurrency holdings in a way that is entirely offline, making it highly secure against online threats. The most common forms of cold storage are hardware wallets and paper wallets.

Hardware Wallets:

Hardware wallets are physical devices designed specifically for securely storing cryptocurrencies.
- They generate and store private keys offline, making them resistant to online attacks.
- Examples include Ledger Nano S, Trezor, and Ledger Nano X.
- To use a hardware wallet, connect it to your computer only when needed for transactions.

Paper Wallets:

A paper wallet is a physical document that contains your cryptocurrency's public and private keys.

- It is generated offline and never exposed to the internet.
- Ensure you create paper wallets using a trusted and secure generator.
- Store paper wallets in a safe, dry place to prevent damage.

Advantages of Cold Storage:

- **High Security:** Cold storage is one of the most secure methods for long-term cryptocurrency storage.
- **Immune to Online Threats:** Since the keys are offline, they are immune to online attacks such as hacking and phishing.

Considerations for Cold Storage:

- **Backup:** Create backups of your cold storage devices or paper wallets to avoid loss due to damage or theft.
- **Ease of Use:** Cold storage is less convenient for frequent transactions, so balance security with accessibility.

3. Regular Updates and Patching

Keeping your software wallets, operating systems, and antivirus programs up-to-date is critical to maintaining a secure environment for your cryptocurrency holdings. Software updates often include security patches that address vulnerabilities.

Advantages of Regular Updates:
- **Security Enhancements:** Updates frequently address known security flaws, protecting your devices from exploitation.
- **Improved Stability:** Updates can enhance the stability and performance of your software.

Implementing Regular Updates:

Enable Automatic Updates: Configure your software and operating systems to install updates automatically.

Check for Updates: Periodically check for updates for all your devices and applications.

Stay Informed: Stay informed about security vulnerabilities related to your software and take action promptly.

4. Strong and Unique Passwords

Creating strong, unique passwords is essential to safeguarding your cryptocurrency accounts. Weak passwords are susceptible to brute force attacks, where attackers systematically guess passwords until they gain access.

Password Best Practices:
- **Complexity:** Use a combination of upper and lower case letters, numbers, and special characters.
- **Length:** Longer passwords are more secure. Aim for at least 12 characters.
- **Avoid Common Words:** Avoid using easily guessable words or phrases.
- **Unique Passwords:** Use different passwords for each cryptocurrency exchange or wallet.

- **Password Manager:** Consider using a reputable password manager to generate and store complex passwords securely.

5. Beware of Phishing Attempts

Phishing attacks are a common threat in the cryptocurrency space. Scammers use deceptive tactics to trick individuals into revealing their private keys or login credentials. Protect yourself by:

- **Verifying URLs:** Always double-check the website's URL before entering sensitive information.
- **Ignore Unsolicited Messages:** Be cautious of unsolicited emails, messages, or social media contacts requesting your private keys or personal information.
- **Use 2FA:** Enable two-factor authentication to add an extra layer of protection against phishing attempts.

Avoiding Scams and Hacks: Tips for recognizing and avoiding potential crypto scams.

Avoiding Scams and Hacks

The cryptocurrency space, while full of opportunities, is rife with scams and hacking attempts. Protecting your investments requires not only securing your wallets but also being vigilant and informed about potential threats. Here are some crucial tips to help you avoid falling victim to scams and hacks:

1. Research Before Investing

Before investing in any cryptocurrency project, conduct thorough research. Scammers often create fake projects, websites, or tokens to lure unsuspecting investors. Here's how to proceed:

- **Check the Project:** Examine the legitimacy of the project by reviewing its whitepaper, team members, and community involvement.
- **Look for Red Flags:** Be cautious if the project promises guaranteed high returns, lacks transparency, or has a poorly designed website.
- **Community Feedback:** Seek feedback from reputable cryptocurrency forums and communities to gauge the project's reputation.

2. Be Wary of Phishing Websites

Phishing websites mimic legitimate cryptocurrency platforms to steal your login credentials or private keys. To avoid falling victim to phishing attacks:

- **Check URLs:** Always verify the website's URL to ensure it matches the official website.
- **Use Bookmarks:** Bookmark cryptocurrency exchange and wallet websites to avoid clicking on phishing links.
- **Use Hardware Wallets:** Hardware wallets are immune to phishing attacks as they require physical confirmation for transactions.

3. Beware of Unsolicited Messages

Scammers often use unsolicited messages via email, social media, or messaging apps to trick individuals into revealing their private keys, passwords, or sending funds. To stay safe:

- **Ignore Unsolicited Requests:** Do not engage with unsolicited messages, especially those requesting sensitive information.
- **Verify Contacts:** Confirm the identity of the sender before responding to any message or request.
- **Use Hardware Wallets:** Hardware wallets require physical confirmation, making it harder for scammers to access your assets remotely.

4. Use Reputable Wallets and Exchanges

Choosing reputable wallets and exchanges is essential. Well-established platforms have security measures in place to protect users from scams and hacks. Here's what to consider:

- **Research Exchanges:** Use exchanges with a track record of security and regulatory compliance.
- **Wallet Selection:** Select wallets that are widely recognized and have a history of security.
- **Regularly Update:** Keep your wallet and exchange software up to date to benefit from the latest security patches.

5. Enable Two-Factor Authentication (2FA)

Two-factor authentication adds an extra layer of security to your accounts by requiring two forms of verification before granting access. Always enable 2FA on your exchange and wallet accounts:

- **Use App-Based 2FA:** Whenever possible, use app-based 2FA methods like Google Authenticator, as SMS-based 2FA can be vulnerable to SIM swapping attacks.

6. Avoid Investment Schemes and Unrealistic Promises

Be cautious of investment schemes that promise guaranteed high returns or use terms like "get rich quick." These are often scams designed to lure unsuspecting investors:

- **Use Caution:** Exercise caution when presented with investment opportunities that seem too good to be true.
- **Diversify Investments:** Avoid putting all your funds into a single investment, as this can mitigate potential losses.

7. Keep Your Private Keys Secure

Your private keys are the keys to your cryptocurrency holdings. Keep them safe by following these guidelines:

- **Do Not Share:** Never share your private keys with anyone, even if they claim to be a support representative.
- **Use Hardware Wallets:** Hardware wallets securely store your private keys offline, reducing the risk of theft.

8. Stay Informed and Educated

Staying informed about the latest cryptocurrency scams and hacks is crucial. Knowledge is your best defense. Here's how to stay educated:

- **Follow Reputable Sources:** Stay updated on cryptocurrency news from reputable sources.
- **Learn from Others:** Engage in cryptocurrency communities and forums to learn from others' experiences.

- **Ask Questions:** When in doubt, seek advice and ask questions about potential scams in cryptocurrency communities.

9. Report Suspected Scams

If you come across a potential scam or fraudulent activity, report it to the relevant authorities or cryptocurrency platforms. Reporting can help protect others from falling victim to the same scams.

Chapter 6: Regulatory Landscape

As the cryptocurrency ecosystem continues to evolve, so does the legal and regulatory framework governing it. Let's explore the evolving landscape of global cryptocurrency regulations.

Global Regulations: Exploring the evolving legal and regulatory framework for cryptocurrencies.

Global Regulations

Cryptocurrencies have garnered significant attention from governments and regulators worldwide. While regulations differ from one country to another, some common trends and challenges shape the global regulatory landscape:

1. Recognition as Legal Assets

One of the primary concerns for regulators has been whether to recognize cryptocurrencies as legal assets. Some countries have embraced cryptocurrencies as a legal means of exchange, while others remain cautious. The recognition of cryptocurrencies varies:

- **Legal Tender:** In some countries like El Salvador, cryptocurrencies like Bitcoin have been recognized as legal tender, allowing citizens to use them for everyday transactions.
- **Commodity:** In the United States, cryptocurrencies are often treated as commodities by regulatory authorities like the Commodity Futures Trading Commission (CFTC).
- **Securities:** Certain cryptocurrencies and initial coin offerings (ICOs) have been categorized as securities by regulators in various countries, subjecting them to securities laws.

2. Anti-Money Laundering (AML) and Know Your Customer (KYC) Regulations

To combat illegal activities such as money laundering and terrorist financing, many countries have implemented AML and KYC regulations for cryptocurrency exchanges and service providers:

- **Verification Requirements:** Exchanges are often required to verify the identities of their users, implementing KYC procedures similar to traditional financial institutions.
- **Transaction Monitoring:** Regulatory authorities may require exchanges to monitor and report suspicious transactions.

3. Taxation

Cryptocurrency taxation is a complex issue. Regulations regarding the taxation of cryptocurrencies vary widely between countries:

- **Income Tax:** In some countries, cryptocurrencies are subject to income tax, and individuals must report gains or losses from cryptocurrency transactions.
- **Capital Gains Tax:** Other nations treat cryptocurrency gains as capital gains, with tax rates often varying based on the duration of the holding period.
- **Value Added Tax (VAT):** Some countries impose VAT on the purchase or sale of cryptocurrencies, while others exempt them from VAT.

4. Securities Regulations

Regulators in various countries closely scrutinize ICOs and tokens to determine whether they should be classified as securities. Regulatory agencies like the U.S. Securities and Exchange Commission (SEC) have issued guidelines on this matter:

- **Utility Tokens vs. Security Tokens:** The classification of a token as a utility token or a security token can have significant regulatory implications.
- **Registration Requirements:** Security tokens may be subject to registration with regulatory authorities and compliance with securities laws.

5. Consumer Protection

To protect consumers, regulators often focus on issues such as fraud, scams, and the transparency of cryptocurrency projects:

- **Fraud Prevention:** Authorities take action against fraudulent cryptocurrency schemes and unregistered investment products.
- **Transparency:** Regulatory agencies may require cryptocurrency projects to provide clear and accurate information to investors.

6. Exchange Regulations

Cryptocurrency exchanges, which act as intermediaries for buying and selling cryptocurrencies, are subject to regulations:

- **Licensing:** Some countries require cryptocurrency exchanges to obtain licenses and adhere to specific operational and security standards.
- **Market Surveillance:** Regulatory authorities may implement market surveillance measures to detect and prevent market manipulation and abusive trading practices.

7. Cross-Border Challenges

Cryptocurrencies operate across borders, making global regulatory coordination challenging:

- **Jurisdictional Discrepancies:** Different countries have varying regulatory approaches to cryptocurrencies, leading to jurisdictional discrepancies.

- **Global Regulatory Cooperation:** Efforts are underway to foster international cooperation among regulators to address cross-border challenges effectively.

8. Evolving Regulations

The regulatory landscape is continually evolving as regulators adapt to the rapidly changing cryptocurrency space. Some countries are actively working on comprehensive regulatory frameworks to address emerging challenges.

Impact on Investments: Discussing how regulations can affect your investments and trading.

Impact on Investments

Cryptocurrency investments are not insulated from the influence of regulatory frameworks. Here, we delve into the various ways in which regulations can affect your investments:

1. Market Stability

Regulatory actions can significantly impact market stability. Positive regulations that provide clarity and protection can attract institutional investors and enhance market stability. Conversely, sudden and stringent regulations can lead to market volatility and price fluctuations.

- **Investor Confidence:** Clear and reasonable regulations can instill confidence in investors, attracting institutional players and fostering a more stable market environment.
- **Price Volatility:** Uncertainty stemming from regulatory developments can lead to price

volatility as investors react to news and regulatory changes.

2. Access to Exchanges

Regulations can affect your ability to access cryptocurrency exchanges. Some regions may impose restrictions on exchanges, limiting your options for trading and investing.

- **Exchange Restrictions:** Regulatory authorities may impose restrictions on cryptocurrency exchanges, leading to reduced availability or functionality for users in certain jurisdictions.
- **Exclusion of Tokens:** Certain tokens or cryptocurrencies may be delisted or become inaccessible due to regulatory concerns.

3. Compliance Requirements

Regulatory compliance often necessitates additional steps and costs for investors and traders. Understanding and adhering to these requirements is essential:

- **Identity Verification:** KYC and AML requirements may necessitate identity verification, which can be time-consuming and intrusive.
- **Reporting Obligations:** Investors may be required to report their cryptocurrency holdings and transactions for tax purposes, adding to the administrative burden.

4. Tax Implications

Tax regulations for cryptocurrencies can vary widely between jurisdictions. Failure to comply with tax laws can result in penalties or legal consequences:

- **Capital Gains Tax:** Regulations surrounding capital gains tax on cryptocurrency profits can impact the net returns on your investments.
- **Complexity:** Navigating the intricacies of cryptocurrency taxation can be challenging, requiring careful record-keeping and reporting.

5. Security and Custody

Regulations may require exchanges and custodians to adhere to certain security standards to protect user assets. This can have implications for the safety of your investments:

- **Security Measures:** Regulatory requirements may compel exchanges and custodians to implement robust security measures, safeguarding user funds.
- **Third-Party Custody:** Some investors may opt for third-party custody services to comply with regulatory mandates, which may come with associated fees.

6. Initial Coin Offerings (ICOs) and Token Sales

ICOs and token sales are often subject to regulatory scrutiny. Understanding the regulatory environment for such fundraising activities is crucial:

- **Regulatory Compliance:** Complying with securities regulations can affect the viability and legality of ICOs and token sales.
- **Investment Opportunities:** Regulatory actions can impact your ability to participate in certain ICOs or token sales, depending on your jurisdiction.

7. Risk Assessment

Investors must conduct thorough risk assessments, taking into account the regulatory environment in which they operate. Regulatory developments can introduce new risks and uncertainties:

- **Legal Risks:** Failure to comply with regulations can result in legal repercussions, including fines and asset seizures.
- **Market Risks:** Changes in market dynamics driven by regulatory actions can affect the risk profile of your investments.

8. Innovation and Technology Adoption

Regulations can both facilitate and hinder the adoption of innovative technologies in the cryptocurrency space:

- **Innovation Support:** Favorable regulations can promote innovation and the development of new technologies and use cases.
- **Regulatory Hurdles:** Stringent regulations may create barriers to entry for new projects and stifle technological advancements.

9. Investment Strategy Adjustments

Understanding the regulatory landscape is essential for shaping your investment strategy. Depending on your risk tolerance and objectives, you may need to adjust your approach:

- **Long-Term vs. Short-Term:** Regulations may influence whether you opt for long-term "HODLing" or short-term trading strategies.

- **Diversification:** Regulatory considerations may lead to diversification strategies, spreading risk across different asset classes or regions.

10. Global Perspective

Cryptocurrency investments often transcend national borders. Global regulatory developments can impact the international nature of your investments:

Diversified Holdings: Investors may diversify their holdings across multiple jurisdictions to mitigate regulatory risks.

Compliance Challenges: Navigating a patchwork of global regulations can be complex and challenging.

Chapter 7: Beyond Bitcoin: Exploring Altcoins

Altcoins, or alternative cryptocurrencies, are a diverse group of digital assets that have expanded upon the foundations laid by Bitcoin. Let's begin by defining altcoins and examining their multifaceted purposes.

Introduction to Altcoins: Defining altcoins and their purposes beyond a store of value.

Introduction to Altcoins

Altcoins, a portmanteau of "alternative" and "coins," represent a broad category of cryptocurrencies that emerged following the launch of Bitcoin in 2009.

While Bitcoin remains the pioneering cryptocurrency and a widely recognized store of value, altcoins have diversified the cryptocurrency ecosystem, offering innovative features, use cases, and functionalities.

Diverse Purposes Beyond a Store of Value

Unlike Bitcoin, which primarily functions as a digital gold or store of value, altcoins have been designed with various objectives in mind. Let's delve into some of the key purposes that altcoins serve:

1. Smart Contracts and Decentralized Applications (DApps)

Several altcoins, such as Ethereum (ETH), were created to enable smart contracts and decentralized applications (DApps). These digital contracts automatically execute predefined actions when specific conditions are met, without the need for intermediaries. Altcoins supporting smart contracts have opened up a world of possibilities, including automated financial agreements, supply chain management, and more.

2. Privacy and Anonymity

Altcoins like Monero (XMR) and Zcash (ZEC) prioritize user privacy and anonymity. They utilize advanced cryptographic techniques to obfuscate transaction details, offering users greater confidentiality compared to Bitcoin's transparent ledger. These privacy-centric altcoins cater to individuals seeking enhanced financial privacy.

3. Stablecoins

Stablecoins are altcoins designed to maintain a stable value, often pegged to traditional fiat currencies like the US dollar (USD) or commodities like gold.

Tether (USDT) and USD Coin (USDC) are prominent examples. Stablecoins provide a crucial bridge between the volatility of cryptocurrencies and the stability of traditional assets, making them valuable for trading and transferring value.

4. Utility Tokens

Utility tokens, such as Binance Coin (BNB) and Chainlink (LINK), serve specific functions within blockchain ecosystems. They are used to pay for transaction fees, access certain features, or participate in governance decisions. These tokens facilitate the operation of blockchain networks and DApps.

5. Platform Tokens

Some altcoins function as platforms for creating and executing decentralized applications. EOS and Cardano (ADA) are examples of altcoins that offer robust platforms for developers to build DApps. These platforms aim to provide scalability, flexibility, and efficiency for DApp development.

6. Cross-Border Payments

Altcoins like Ripple (XRP) focus on facilitating cross-border payments and remittances. They offer faster and more cost-effective alternatives to traditional financial systems. These altcoins are designed to improve international money transfers by reducing transaction times and fees.

7. Environmental Sustainability

Cryptocurrencies like Chia (XCH) and Tezos (XTZ) explore alternative consensus mechanisms that are more energy-efficient than Bitcoin's Proof of Work (PoW). These altcoins aim to reduce the environmental impact of cryptocurrency mining and offer sustainable alternatives.

8. Niche Use Cases

Some altcoins target niche markets and use cases. For instance, Basic Attention Token (BAT) rewards users for viewing ads on the Brave browser, while VeChain (VET) focuses on supply chain management and product authenticity verification.

9. Experimentation and Innovation

Altcoins provide a platform for experimentation and innovation in the blockchain and cryptocurrency space. Developers and entrepreneurs create new altcoins to test novel concepts, technologies, and governance models, contributing to the ongoing evolution of the crypto ecosystem.

Evaluating Altcoins: Factors to consider when assessing the potential of different altcoins.

Evaluating Altcoins

Altcoins, or alternative cryptocurrencies, come in various forms, each with its unique features, use cases, and growth potential. When evaluating altcoins, it's crucial to adopt a systematic approach that considers both quantitative and qualitative factors. Here are the key aspects to assess:

1. Technology and Innovation

A. **Blockchain Technology:** Examine the underlying blockchain technology. Is it secure, scalable, and efficient? Consider whether the altcoin introduces innovative features or improvements over existing blockchain platforms.

B. **Consensus Mechanism:** Understand the consensus mechanism used by the altcoin. Some use Proof of Work (PoW), while others employ Proof of Stake (PoS) or alternative methods. Assess the efficiency, security, and environmental impact of the chosen mechanism.

C. **Smart Contracts and DApps:** If the altcoin supports smart contracts and decentralized applications (DApps), assess the capabilities and potential use cases of these features. Evaluate developer activity within the ecosystem.

2. Use Case and Utility

A. **Clear Use Case:** Determine whether the altcoin serves a clear and practical use case. Consider whether it solves real-world problems or addresses specific needs in industries such as finance, supply chain, or healthcare.

B. **Adoption and Partnerships:** Investigate whether the altcoin has gained adoption and forged partnerships with businesses or organizations. Real-world utility and adoption are strong indicators of an altcoin's potential.

3. Community and Development

A. **Developer Activity:** Analyze the level of developer activity within the altcoin's ecosystem. Active development teams often lead to ongoing improvements and innovations.

B. **Community Engagement:** Assess the size and engagement of the altcoin community. A passionate and active community can contribute to the altcoin's growth and adoption.

4. Market Dynamics

A. **Market Capitalization:** Consider the altcoin's market capitalization, which reflects its total value. Compare this to Bitcoin and other cryptocurrencies to gauge its relative size and potential for growth.

B. **Liquidity:** Examine the liquidity of the altcoin, which impacts its ease of buying, selling, and trading. Higher liquidity generally indicates a more active market.

C. **Price History and Volatility:** Review the altcoin's price history and volatility. Price stability can be a critical factor for investors, while volatility can present trading opportunities.

5. Regulatory Considerations

A. **Legal Status:** Determine the altcoin's legal status in your jurisdiction. Some countries may have specific regulations governing certain altcoins.

B. **Compliance:** Assess whether the altcoin and its associated projects comply with relevant regulatory requirements, including AML and KYC regulations.

6. Competitive Landscape

A. **Competing Altcoins:** Identify other altcoins with similar use cases and functionalities. Compare the altcoin you're evaluating to its competitors in terms of technology, adoption, and market positioning.

B. **Bitcoin Comparison:** Consider how the altcoin compares to Bitcoin. Some altcoins aim to improve upon Bitcoin's limitations, while others target entirely different use cases.

7. Security and Reliability

A. **Security Measures:** Investigate the altcoin's security measures, including consensus algorithm, network security, and measures against potential attacks or vulnerabilities.

B. **Reliability:** Assess the altcoin's track record for reliability and uptime. Frequent network issues can erode confidence in the cryptocurrency.

8. Roadmap and Future Developments

A. **Roadmap:** Examine the altcoin's roadmap and plans for future developments. A clear and ambitious roadmap can indicate a commitment to ongoing improvement.

B. **Upcoming Features:** Consider any upcoming features or upgrades that may impact the altcoin's utility or adoption.

9. Risk Assessment

A. **Risk Factors:** Identify and evaluate potential risks associated with the altcoin. These may include regulatory risks, technological risks, or market risks.

B. **Mitigation Strategies:** Assess whether the altcoin's team has strategies in place to mitigate identified risks.

10. Long-Term Viability

A. **Long-Term Vision:** Understand the altcoin's long-term vision and goals. Consider whether the altcoin has a clear strategy for achieving these objectives.

B. **Market Resilience:** Assess how the altcoin has weathered past market downturns. Resilience can be an indicator of long-term viability.

Use Cases and Projects: Highlighting specific altcoin projects and their applications.

Use Cases and Projects

Altcoins have expanded the horizon of blockchain technology by introducing a multitude of projects, each designed to address unique challenges and capitalize on specific opportunities. Here, we highlight a selection of noteworthy altcoin projects and their applications.

1. Ethereum (ETH)

Use Case: Smart Contracts and Decentralized Applications (DApps)

Ethereum is perhaps the most well-known altcoin, recognized for its pioneering role in introducing smart contracts and DApps to the blockchain world. Ethereum's blockchain enables developers to create and execute self-executing smart contracts, which automate predefined actions when specific conditions are met. This has led to a wide range of applications, from decentralized finance (DeFi) to non-fungible tokens (NFTs) and supply chain management.

2. Monero (XMR)

Use Case: Privacy and Anonymity

Monero is a privacy-focused altcoin that employs advanced cryptographic techniques to provide enhanced privacy and anonymity for its users.

Unlike Bitcoin, which offers transparent transaction details on its public ledger, Monero transactions are confidential and untraceable. This makes Monero a popular choice for individuals seeking financial privacy.

3. Chainlink (LINK)
Use Case: Oracle Services

Chainlink is an altcoin project that bridges the gap between blockchain smart contracts and real-world data sources. It provides a decentralized oracle network that connects smart contracts with external data feeds, APIs, and payment systems. This enables smart contracts to access real-world information, making Chainlink a critical component for a wide range of applications, including decentralized finance (DeFi) and prediction markets.

4. Binance Coin (BNB)
Use Case: Utility Token

Binance Coin is the native cryptocurrency of the Binance exchange, one of the largest cryptocurrency exchanges in the world. BNB serves various utility functions within the Binance ecosystem, including reduced trading fees, participation in token sales on the Binance Launchpad, and more. Its utility has extended to other platforms and services beyond Binance, making it a versatile altcoin.

5. Ripple (XRP)
Use Case: Cross-Border Payments

Ripple is an altcoin project with a primary focus on facilitating cross-border payments and remittances. Its blockchain technology, known as RippleNet, connects financial institutions and payment providers to enable fast and cost-effective international money transfers. Ripple's native token, XRP, is used to facilitate these transactions, offering an alternative to the traditional correspondent banking system.

6. VeChain (VET)
Use Case: Supply Chain Management

VeChain is an altcoin project designed to improve supply chain management and product authenticity verification. It utilizes blockchain technology to track and trace products throughout the supply chain, enhancing transparency and reducing counterfeiting. VeChain's applications extend to industries like agriculture, luxury goods, and pharmaceuticals.

7. Tezos (XTZ)
Use Case: Smart Contracts and Governance

Tezos is an altcoin project that combines smart contract capabilities with an innovative self-amendment system. It allows token holders to propose and vote on upgrades and changes to the protocol, enabling on-chain governance. Tezos' approach to governance and its ability to evolve through community consensus make it an intriguing altcoin project.

8. Cardano (ADA)
Use Case: Smart Contracts and Sustainability

Cardano is an altcoin project known for its focus on sustainability and scalability. It offers a platform for the development of smart contracts and DApps. Cardano aims to provide a more energy-efficient alternative to blockchain consensus mechanisms, making it an attractive choice for environmentally conscious projects.

9. Basic Attention Token (BAT)
Use Case: Digital Advertising

Basic Attention Token is an altcoin project that seeks to revolutionize the digital advertising industry. It operates within the Brave browser ecosystem, where users are rewarded with BAT for viewing privacy-respecting ads. This innovative approach aims to create a fairer and more efficient digital advertising ecosystem.

10. Chia (XCH)
Use Case: Sustainable Mining

Chia is an altcoin project that addresses the environmental concerns associated with traditional Proof of Work (PoW) mining. Chia introduces a consensus mechanism called Proof of Space and Time (PoST), which relies on available disk space rather than energy-intensive computations. This sustainable approach to mining aims to reduce the environmental impact of cryptocurrency networks.

Chapter 8: The Future of Cryptocurrencies

We will explore the future of cryptocurrencies, with a specific focus on ongoing technological advancements and innovations that are shaping the crypto space.

Technological Advancements: Discussing ongoing developments and innovations in the crypto space.

We will explore the future of cryptocurrencies, with a specific focus on ongoing technological advancements and innovations that are shaping the crypto space.

Technological Advancements

Cryptocurrencies have come a long way since the inception of Bitcoin in 2009. As we look ahead, it's evident that the crypto space is poised for further technological evolution. Here are some of the ongoing technological advancements that hold the key to the future of cryptocurrencies:

1. Scalability Solutions

    A. **Layer 2 Scaling:** Layer 2 scaling solutions like the Lightning Network for Bitcoin and similar solutions for other blockchains aim to enhance transaction throughput and reduce fees. These off-chain protocols enable faster and more cost-effective transactions, making cryptocurrencies more practical for everyday use.

B. **Sharding:** Sharding is a technique that partitions a blockchain into smaller, more manageable segments called "shards." Each shard processes a subset of transactions, significantly improving scalability. Ethereum 2.0 is one prominent blockchain adopting sharding to boost performance.

2. Interoperability

A. **Cross-Chain Compatibility:** Interoperability solutions aim to facilitate seamless communication and asset transfer between different blockchain networks. Projects like Polkadot and Cosmos are working on interoperability protocols, allowing assets and data to move freely between blockchains.

3. Privacy Enhancements

A. **Zero-Knowledge Proofs:** Zero-knowledge proofs, such as zk-SNARKs and zk-STARKs, enable users to prove the truth of a statement without revealing the underlying data. These privacy-enhancing technologies are being integrated into various cryptocurrencies to provide improved confidentiality and data protection.

4. Consensus Mechanisms

A. **Proof of Stake (PoS):** PoS consensus mechanisms, which rely on validators holding and staking cryptocurrency as collateral, are becoming more prevalent. They offer energy efficiency and lower environmental impact compared to traditional Proof of Work (PoW) systems.

B. **Delegated Proof of Stake (DPoS):** DPoS combines PoS with a delegated voting system, where token holders select a limited number of trusted validators to confirm transactions. This approach enhances scalability and reduces centralization risks.

5. Cross-Platform Integrations

A. **DeFi Integration:** Decentralized finance (DeFi) platforms are increasingly integrating with various blockchains, expanding the range of financial services available to users. These integrations enable assets to flow seamlessly between DeFi applications and different blockchains.

6. Quantum Resistance

A. **Quantum Computing Defense:** The emergence of quantum computing poses a potential threat to current encryption methods used in cryptocurrencies. To address this, quantum-resistant cryptographic algorithms are being developed to secure blockchain networks against quantum attacks.

7. Smart Contract Languages

A. **Advanced Smart Contract Languages:** New smart contract programming languages and tools are being developed to make it easier for developers to create complex and secure smart contracts. These advancements aim to reduce vulnerabilities and improve the reliability of smart contracts.

8. Decentralized Autonomous Organizations (DAOs)

A. **Governance Models:** DAOs are gaining traction as decentralized organizations governed by token holders. Future advancements in DAO technology may enable more sophisticated and efficient decision-making processes, further decentralizing control.

9. Cross-Asset Capabilities

A. **Tokenization of Assets:** The tokenization of real-world assets, such as real estate and art, is on the rise. This enables fractional ownership, increased liquidity, and efficient trading of traditionally illiquid assets.

10. Energy Efficiency

A. **Green Mining Solutions:** Cryptocurrencies are exploring environmentally friendly mining solutions, including renewable energy sources and more energy-efficient consensus mechanisms. These efforts aim to reduce the carbon footprint of blockchain networks.

11. Regulatory Compliance

A. **Privacy Coins and Regulation:** Some privacy-focused cryptocurrencies are developing features to allow selective transparency and regulatory compliance while preserving user privacy. This may help address regulatory concerns regarding anonymity.

12. Cross-Border Payments

A. **CBDC Integration:** Central bank digital currencies (CBDCs) may integrate with existing cryptocurrencies to facilitate cross-border payments and improve financial inclusion on a global scale.

13. Education and User-Friendly Tools

A. **Widespread Adoption:** Ongoing efforts to educate users about cryptocurrencies and provide user-friendly tools and interfaces aim to drive widespread adoption. This includes mobile wallets, intuitive trading platforms, and educational resources.

Mainstream Adoption: Exploring the potential for cryptocurrencies to become widely accepted.

Mainstream Adoption

The journey toward mainstream adoption of cryptocurrencies has been marked by both progress and challenges. As we look ahead, several factors indicate the growing potential for cryptocurrencies to become widely accepted on a global scale.

1. Digital Transformation

A. **Changing Financial Landscape:** The ongoing digitization of financial services is reshaping the way people manage their money. Mobile banking, contactless payments, and digital wallets have become increasingly common, setting the stage for the acceptance of digital currencies.

B. **Economic Inclusion:** Cryptocurrencies have the potential to provide financial services to unbanked and underbanked populations worldwide. By enabling access to banking services via smartphones, cryptocurrencies can promote economic inclusion.

2. Institutional Investment

A. **Institutional Interest:** Large financial institutions, including banks and investment firms, are showing growing interest in cryptocurrencies. Institutional investment not only brings credibility to the crypto space but also paves the way for more comprehensive financial products and services.

B. **Regulatory Clarity:** Regulatory clarity, as it pertains to institutional involvement, is crucial. Clear and well-defined regulations can provide institutions with the confidence needed to engage with cryptocurrencies.

3. Global Payments and Remittances

A. **Cross-Border Payments:** Cryptocurrencies offer a more efficient and cost-effective solution for cross-border payments and remittances. Their ability to facilitate near-instantaneous transactions across borders can reduce the time and fees associated with traditional banking methods.

B. **Financial Inclusion:** Cross-border payments are particularly relevant for individuals in regions with limited access to traditional banking services. Cryptocurrencies can bridge this gap and foster financial inclusion.

4. Retail Adoption

A. **Merchant Acceptance:** The acceptance of cryptocurrencies by retailers and e-commerce platforms is expanding. This allows consumers to use digital currencies for everyday purchases, further integrating cryptocurrencies into daily life.

B. **Cryptocurrency ATMs:** The proliferation of cryptocurrency ATMs worldwide makes it easier for individuals to buy and sell digital assets with fiat currency.

5. Government Initiatives

A. **Central Bank Digital Currencies (CBDCs):** Several countries are exploring the development of CBDCs, which are government-backed digital currencies. These initiatives aim to provide a secure and regulated digital alternative to physical cash.

B. **Regulatory Frameworks:** Governments are working to establish clear regulatory frameworks for cryptocurrencies, striking a balance between innovation and consumer protection. Well-defined regulations can foster trust and acceptance.

6. Educational Initiatives

A. **Cryptocurrency Education:** Educational programs and initiatives are helping to raise awareness and understanding of cryptocurrencies among the general public.

These efforts reduce the learning curve and skepticism associated with digital assets.

B. **User-Friendly Interfaces:** User-friendly cryptocurrency wallets and platforms are becoming more prevalent, making it easier for individuals to navigate the world of digital assets.

7. Financial Innovation

A. **DeFi:** The decentralized finance (DeFi) movement is revolutionizing traditional financial services, offering users access to lending, borrowing, trading, and more without intermediaries. DeFi has the potential to attract a broader audience to cryptocurrencies.

B. **NFTs:** Non-fungible tokens (NFTs) are gaining popularity in art, gaming, and entertainment. These unique digital assets could serve as a gateway for newcomers to explore the broader cryptocurrency space.

8. Market Maturity

a. Stability and Liquidity: The cryptocurrency market has matured significantly, with increased stability and liquidity. Reduced volatility can encourage broader adoption as users feel more confident in the asset class.

b. Diverse Investment Options: A wide range of cryptocurrencies and investment options has emerged, allowing users to tailor their portfolios to their preferences and risk tolerance.

9. Security and Custody Solutions

    A. **Security Measures:** Advancements in cryptocurrency security, including hardware wallets and multi-signature wallets, provide users with safer ways to store and manage their digital assets.

    B. **Custody Services:** Institutional-grade custody services are becoming more accessible, addressing concerns about the safekeeping of digital assets.

10. Market Awareness and Perception

    A. **Media Coverage:** Extensive media coverage has raised awareness of cryptocurrencies and their potential benefits. Positive narratives surrounding the technology can influence public perception.

    B. **Use Cases:** Demonstrating real-world use cases beyond speculative trading can help individuals understand the practical applications of cryptocurrencies.

Long-Term Prospects: Delving into the possible trajectory of the crypto market in the coming years.

Long-Term Prospects

As we contemplate the future of cryptocurrencies, it becomes evident that digital assets are here to stay. While the market's short-term volatility is a characteristic feature, the long-term outlook for cryptocurrencies appears promising, driven by several key factors.

1. **Global Adoption**
   A. **Emerging Markets:** Cryptocurrencies are gaining traction in emerging markets where traditional banking infrastructure may be less robust. These regions could become significant hubs for cryptocurrency adoption.
   B. **Currency Crises:** In regions plagued by currency instability or hyperinflation, cryptocurrencies offer a reliable store of value and a means of preserving wealth.
2. **Financial Inclusion**
   A. **Unbanked Populations:** Cryptocurrencies provide unbanked populations with access to financial services, allowing individuals to participate in the global economy without relying on traditional banks.
   B. **Microtransactions:** Cryptocurrencies enable microtransactions and small-scale financial activities that were previously uneconomical with traditional banking systems.
3. **Diversification of Portfolios**
   A. **Asset Diversification:** As cryptocurrencies mature and become recognized as a legitimate asset class, investors are increasingly including digital assets in their diversified portfolios to reduce risk and enhance returns.
   B. **Hedge Against Inflation:** Cryptocurrencies, particularly Bitcoin, are seen as hedges against inflation and economic uncertainty. This perception may further drive investment.

4. Blockchain Technology

A. **Beyond Cryptocurrencies:** Blockchain technology has applications beyond cryptocurrencies, including supply chain management, healthcare, voting systems, and more. Continued innovation in these areas could further fuel the adoption of blockchain-based solutions.

B. **Smart Contracts:** The use of smart contracts can streamline business operations by automating agreements and reducing the need for intermediaries.

5. Regulatory Clarity

A. **Established Frameworks:** Clear and well-defined regulatory frameworks provide businesses and investors with confidence in the cryptocurrency space. Regulatory clarity can pave the way for broader adoption.

B. **Institutional Investment:** Institutional investors, such as pension funds and endowments, are more likely to enter the cryptocurrency market when regulatory concerns are addressed.

6. Technological Advancements

A. **Scalability:** Ongoing efforts to enhance blockchain scalability can lead to faster, more efficient, and cost-effective cryptocurrency transactions, making digital assets more attractive for everyday use.

B. **Privacy Enhancements:** Advances in privacy-enhancing technologies can address concerns about data protection and user privacy in cryptocurrency transactions.

7. Education and Awareness

A. **Widespread Knowledge:** Increased education and awareness campaigns help demystify cryptocurrencies and make them more accessible to the general public.

B. **User-Friendly Interfaces:** User-friendly cryptocurrency wallets and platforms are making it easier for individuals to interact with digital assets.

8. Market Maturation

A. **Stability:** As the cryptocurrency market matures, reduced volatility can attract a broader audience of investors and users.

B. **Diverse Investment Options:** The availability of a wide range of cryptocurrencies and investment options caters to various preferences and risk profiles.

9. Geopolitical Factors

A. **Digital Sovereignty:** Governments may explore the development of their digital currencies, emphasizing digital sovereignty. These state-backed digital currencies could coexist with existing cryptocurrencies.

B. **Global Competition:** Competition among nations to establish themselves as leaders in blockchain and cryptocurrency technology can foster innovation and adoption.

10. Evolution of Use Cases

A. **Expanding Use Cases:** Cryptocurrencies are finding applications in sectors beyond finance, including healthcare, real estate, and the arts. The evolution of these use cases can drive adoption.

B. **Integration with Traditional Finance:** Cryptocurrencies are becoming increasingly integrated with traditional financial systems, allowing for smoother transitions between fiat and digital assets.

11. Environmental Sustainability

A. **Green Initiatives:** As environmental concerns rise, the cryptocurrency industry is exploring greener alternatives, such as sustainable mining practices and energy-efficient consensus mechanisms.

B. **Carbon Offset:** Some cryptocurrency projects are taking steps to offset their carbon emissions, addressing concerns about the environmental impact of blockchain networks.

12. Long-Term Vision

A. **Innovative Projects:** Continued development of innovative projects with long-term visions can keep the cryptocurrency space dynamic and relevant.

B. **Resilience:** The cryptocurrency market has demonstrated resilience in the face of challenges, which can instill confidence in its long-term prospects.

Conclusion: Navigating the Crypto Journey

In this comprehensive journey through the world of digital investments, we have embarked on a quest to unravel the complexities of cryptocurrencies, blockchain technology, and the evolving landscape of digital assets. As we draw our exploration to a close, it is crucial to revisit the key takeaways, inspire action, and emphasize the ever-evolving nature of the crypto space.

Key Takeaways

Throughout this book, we have uncovered valuable insights into the realm of cryptocurrencies:

- **Education is Fundamental:** A solid understanding of blockchain technology and cryptocurrencies is the foundation upon which successful investments are built. Take the time to learn, question, and explore.
- **Diverse Ecosystem:** The cryptocurrency ecosystem is vast and multifaceted. Beyond Bitcoin, a world of altcoins, each with its unique use cases, beckons exploration.
- **Blockchain's Promise:** Blockchain technology extends far beyond digital currencies. Its potential to revolutionize industries, enhance transparency, and facilitate trust is immense.

- **Investment Caution:** Crypto investments are inherently risky. Assessing risk and conducting due diligence are paramount to making informed decisions.
- **Strategy Matters:** Different investment strategies, such as trading or holding, suit different goals and risk tolerances. Tailor your approach to align with your objectives.
- **Security is Non-Negotiable:** Safeguarding your digital assets through secure wallets and practices is imperative in the crypto world, where security breaches can have severe consequences.
- **Regulatory Awareness:** Regulations continue to evolve. Staying informed about the legal landscape in your region is vital to mitigate regulatory risks.
- **Altcoin Exploration:** Altcoins present opportunities beyond Bitcoin. Explore the diverse world of digital assets, but do so with a discerning eye.
- **The Role of Exchanges:** Crypto exchanges serve as the gateways to the digital asset world. Choose reputable and secure platforms to facilitate your investments.
- **The Future of Cryptocurrencies:** The long-term prospects for cryptocurrencies are promising, driven by global adoption, technological advancements, and financial innovation.

Start Your Journey

As we wrap up this exploration, it's essential to encourage you to take action. Whether you're a novice or a seasoned investor, the crypto landscape offers opportunities for all. Begin your journey with newfound clarity and caution:

- **Educate Yourself:** Knowledge is your most potent weapon in the crypto world. Dive deeper, ask questions, and continue learning as the industry evolves.
- **Start Small:** Begin your investment journey with a cautious approach. Dip your toes into the market, experiment, and gain confidence over time.
- **Diversify Wisely:** Diversification can mitigate risk. Explore different cryptocurrencies and investment strategies to balance your portfolio effectively.
- **Seek Guidance:** Engage with the crypto community, attend conferences, and seek the advice of experienced investors. Learning from others can expedite your growth.
- **Stay Secure:** Prioritize security. Use reputable wallets, enable two-factor authentication, and follow best practices to protect your digital assets.
- **Embrace Regulatory Compliance:** Understand and adhere to the regulatory environment in your jurisdiction. Compliance

ensures you operate within the bounds of the law.

Ongoing Evolution

In closing, it's vital to recognize that the cryptocurrency landscape is in a perpetual state of evolution. The lessons learned today may evolve tomorrow. The strategies that work today may require adjustment in the future. Staying informed, adaptive, and resilient is key to success.

As you embark on your crypto investment journey, remember that clarity and caution will be your guiding stars. Keep an eye on the horizon, embrace change, and seize opportunities as they arise. With diligence, knowledge, and a measured approach, you are well-equipped to navigate the ever-shifting currents of the digital investment world.

Thank you for joining us on this enlightening expedition through Crypto Clarity. May your path in the world of digital investments be illuminated, your decisions informed, and your journey filled with prosperity and wisdom.

www.ingramcontent.com/pod-product-compliance
Lightning Source LLC
LaVergne TN
LVHW051715050326
832903LV00032B/4216